Traditional and Modern

Recipes from Laos

A Collection of Authentic and Contemporary Lao
Dishes

BY

Alex Aton

-■-■-■-■-■-■-■-■-■-■-■-■-■-■-■

Licensing Information

It is strictly prohibited to engage in any commercial or non-commercial activity related to the content of this book without the explicit permission of the author. This includes, but is not limited to, selling, publishing, printing, copying, disseminating, or distributing the content in any form or medium. The author holds exclusive rights to the content and reserves the right to take legal action against any unauthorized usage.

If you have obtained an illegal copy of this book, please delete it immediately and obtain a legal version. Purchasing a legal version of this book supports the author's hard work and dedication in creating the content.

However, the author does not take responsibility for any actions taken by the reader based on the information provided in the book. The content is intended solely as an informational tool and the author has taken all necessary steps to ensure its accuracy. However, as with any information source, caution must be exercised when taking any steps based on the content of this book. It is advisable to seek professional guidance before taking any significant actions based on the information provided in this book.

■-■-■-■-■-■-■-■-■-■-■-■-■-■-■-■

Table of Contents

Introduction

Welcome to the enchanting world of Lao cuisine and our cookbook, "Traditional and Modern Recipes from Laos." Lao cooking is a rich tapestry of flavors, cultural heritage, and regional diversity that captivates food lovers worldwide. Lao cuisine uses a variety of aromatic herbs, spices, and fresh ingredients, resulting in dishes that are both flavorful and visually appealing.

Our cookbook embodies the authentic and traditional dishes of Laos while also offering innovative and modern twists. It combines the finest ingredients with easy-to-follow instructions, encouraging novice and expert chefs alike to cook and enjoy the flavors of Laos.

"Traditional and Modern Recipes from Laos" takes you on a culinary journey through the vibrant markets, bustling street food stalls, and home kitchens of Laos. We bring you a collection of carefully curated recipes, ranging from the most iconic and celebrated dishes of Lao cuisine to lesser-known regional gems.

Whether you're a seasoned cook, an aspiring chef, or simply a lover of food and culture, "Traditional and Modern Recipes from Laos" is a must-have companion and guidebook to the delectable world of Lao cuisine. Discover the unique and complex flavors that define Lao cooking and elevate your culinary creations with our cookbook.

XXXXXXXXXXXXXXXXXXXXXXXXX

1. Ping Gai (Grilled chicken)

Ping Gai is a popular Lao dish consisting of grilled chicken marinated with lemongrass, garlic, and other herbs and spices. The chicken is typically cut into bite-size pieces and served with a dipping sauce made of jeow bong, a spicy and sweet chili paste. The chicken is often accompanied by a side of sticky rice and sliced cucumber and lettuce. With its fragrant aroma and juicy, flavorful meat, Ping Gai is a delectable and beloved dish that captures the essence of Lao cuisine.

Preparation Time: 25 min

Serving size: 2

Ingredients:

- 2 chicken breasts
- 2 tablespoons soy sauce
- 2 tablespoons fish sauce
- 2 tablespoons oyster sauce
- 1 tablespoon honey
- 1 tablespoon vegetable oil
- 2 cloves garlic, minced.
- 1 teaspoon ginger, grated.
- 1 tablespoon lime juice
- Salt and pepper to taste.

xxxxxxxxxxxxxxxxxxxxxxxxxx

Instructions:

a) In a mixing bowl, combine the soy sauce, fish sauce, oyster sauce, honey, vegetable oil, minced garlic, grated ginger, lime juice, salt, and pepper.

b) Add the chicken breasts to the marinade and let them marinate for at least 15 minutes.

c) Preheat a grill pan or outdoor grill over medium-high heat.

d) Grill the chicken breasts for about 6-8 minutes each side, or until they reach an inside temperature of 165°F (74°C).

e) Remove the chicken from the grill and let it rest for a few minutes before slicing.

f) Serve the Ping Gai - Grilled Chicken with your favorite side dishes, such as steamed rice or salad.

2. Laap (Spicy minced meat salad)

Laap is a classic Lao dish known for its bold and vibrant flavors. This spicy minced meat salad is traditionally made with either pork, beef, or chicken, along with a mixture of fresh herbs, lime juice, fish sauce, chili, and toasted rice powder. The combination of tangy, savory, and slightly spicy flavors creates a harmonious balance that is both refreshing and satisfying. Served alongside sticky rice and fresh vegetables, Laap is a delicious and iconic dish that showcases the essence of Lao cuisine.

Preparation Time: 25 min

Serving size: 2

Ingredients:

- 1 lb. ground meat (chicken, beef, pork, or lamb)
- 2 shallots thinly sliced.
- 2 green onions, chopped.
- 1/4 cup fresh lime juice
- 2 tablespoons fish sauce
- 1 tablespoon rice powder
- 1 tablespoon chili flakes (adjust to your desired level of spiciness)
- Fresh herbs (such as mint, cilantro, and Thai basil), chopped.
- Lettuce leaves for serving.

XXXXXXXXXXXXXXXXXXXXXXXXX

Instructions:

a) Heat a large pan over medium heat and add the ground meat. Cook until the meat is fully cooked and browned, breaking it up into small pieces with a spatula.

b) While the meat is cooking, toast the rice powder in a dry pan over medium heat until it turns golden brown and fragrant. Remove from heat and set aside.

c) In a mixing bowl, combine the cooked ground meat, shallots, green onions, lime juice, fish sauce, rice powder, and chili flakes. Mix well to combine all the flavors.

d) Taste the mixture and adjust the seasoning if needed, by adding more lime juice, fish sauce, or chili flakes according to your preference.

e) Add the chopped fresh herbs to the bowl and mix gently to incorporate them into the meat mixture.

f) Let the salad sit for about 10-15 minutes to allow the flavors to meld together.

g) To serve, place lettuce leaves on a plate or individual bowls. Spoon the laap mixture onto the lettuce leaves.

h) Garnish with additional herbs and lime wedges, if desired.

i) Enjoy the delicious and spicy Laap salad by wrapping the flavorful meat mixture in the lettuce leaves.

3. Tam Mak Hoong - Spicy Green Papaya Salad

Tam Mak Hoong, also well known as spicy green papaya salad, is a staple in Lao cuisine. This vibrant salad is made with cut up green papaya, tomatoes, carrots, lime juice, fish sauce, chili, and often includes ingredients like green beans, garlic, and peanuts. The result is a medley of flavors that is sour, salty, spicy, and slightly sweet. Tam Mak Hoong is refreshing, light, and packs a punch of heat, making it a popular choice as a side dish or appetizer in Lao cuisine.

Preparation Time: 25 min

Serving size: 2

Ingredients:

- 2 cloves of garlic
- 5 cherry tomatoes
- 1 green papaya
- 2 Thai chili peppers
- 2 tablespoons of fish sauce
- 1 tablespoon of lime juice
- 1 tablespoon of palm sugar
- 2 tablespoons of roasted peanuts
- Fresh cilantro leaves for garnish

XXXXXXXXXXXXXXXXXXXXXXXXXX

Instructions:

a) Peel the green papaya and grate it into thin strips.

b) In a mortar, crush the garlic and chili peppers together.

c) Add the cherry tomatoes and lightly crush them.

d) Add the fish sauce, lime juice, and palm sugar to the mortar and mix well.

e) In a mixing bowl, combine the grated papaya and the mixture from the mortar.

f) Toss the salad well, making sure the dressing coats all the papaya.

g) Serve the salad on a plate and sprinkle with roasted peanuts.

h) Garnish with fresh cilantro leaves.

4. Larb Moo - Spicy minced pork salad

Larb Moo is a mouth-watering Lao salad that features spicy minced pork and fresh herbs. The pork is seasoned with fish sauce, lime juice, and chili, and then stir-fried until cooked. It is then combined with herbs including mint, cilantro, and green onions, and garnished with toasted rice powder for added texture. Served with sticky rice and lettuce leaves, Larb Moo is a deliciously unique salad that has bold and zesty flavors that are both satisfying and addictive, making it a must-try dish in Lao cuisine.

Preparation Time: 25 min

Serving size: 2

Ingredients:

- minced pork
- lime juice
- fish sauce
- shallots
- mint leaves
- coriander leaves
- chili flakes
- rice powder
- lettuce leaves

XXXXXXXXXXXXXXXXXXXXXXXXX

Instructions:

a) In a pan, cook the minced pork until browned.

b) In a mixing bowl, combine lime juice, fish sauce, shallots, mint leaves, coriander leaves, and chili flakes.

c) Add the cooked minced pork into the mixing bowl and mix well.

d) Sprinkle rice powder over the salad mixture and toss to combine.

e) Serve the Larb Moo on lettuce leaves.

5. Sai Oua - Lao sausage

Sai Oua, also known as Lao sausage, is a flavorful and aromatic dish that is popular in Laos. Made from ground pork mixed with lemongrass, galangal, kaffir lime leaves, and a variety of spices, this sausage is known for its distinctive herbal taste. Grilled or pan-fried to perfection, Sai Oua is juicy and packed with bold flavors. It is often served as an appetizer or as part of a main course and is a beloved dish that highlights the rich and diverse flavors of Lao cuisine.

Preparation Time: 25 min

Serving size: 2

Ingredients:

- 500g ground pork
- 2 lemongrass stalks
- 4 kaffir lime leaves
- 3 shallots
- 4 cloves garlic
- 1 tablespoon galangal
- 1 tablespoon fish sauce
- 1 tablespoon soy sauce
- 1 teaspoon sugar
- 1 teaspoon salt
- 1 teaspoon chili flakes
- 1/2 teaspoon black pepper

XXXXXXXXXXXXXXXXXXXXXXXXXX

Instructions:

a) Finely chop the lemongrass stalks, kaffir lime leaves, shallots, and garlic.

b) In a mortar and pestle, pound the chopped lemongrass, kaffir lime leaves, shallots, garlic, and galangal into a paste.

c) In a bowl, merge the ground pork, lemongrass paste, fish sauce, soy sauce, sugar, salt, chili flakes, and black pepper.

d) Mix well until all the ingredients are evenly incorporated.

e) Divide the mixture into 2 equal portions and shape them into sausages.

f) Preheat a grill pan over medium heat and cook the sausages for about 10-12 minutes, turning regularly, until they are cooked evenly and have a nice char on the outside.

g) Remove from heat and let them rest for a few minutes before serving.

6. Mok Pa - Steamed fish in banana leaves

Mok Pa, also known as fish, steamed in banana leaves, is a traditional Lao dish. The fish is finely chopped and then mixed with herbs such as lemongrass, galangal, and kaffir lime leaves, as well as chili paste, fish sauce, and coconut milk. The mixture is then wrapped in banana leaves and steamed until cooked. The resulting dish is moist, fragrant, and full of flavor, with a delicate texture that is both comforting and satisfying. Mok Pa is a must-try dish for anyone looking to experience the delicious flavors of Lao cuisine.

Preparation Time: 25 min

Serving size: 2

Ingredients:

- 2 fish fillets
- 4 kaffir lime leaves
- 2 stalks lemongrass
- 2 tablespoons fish sauce
- 1 tablespoon lime juice
- 1 tablespoon chopped cilantro.
- 1 tablespoon chopped green onions.
- 1 red chili, sliced.
- Banana leaves for wrapping.

XXXXXXXXXXXXXXXXXXXXXXXXXX

Instructions:

a) Clean and pat dry the fish fillets.

b) Slice the lemongrass stalks into thin strips.

c) In a bowl, mix together fish sauce, lime juice, cilantro, green onions, and sliced chili.

d) Place a piece of banana leaf on a flat surface.

e) Put a fish fillet on top of the banana leaf.

f) Spread some of the sauce mixture on top of the fish fillet.

g) Add some kaffir lime leaves and lemongrass strips on top.

h) Fold the banana leaf to wrap the fish fillet tightly.

i) Repeat steps 4-8 for the second fish fillet.

j) Place the wrapped fish fillets in a steaming pot.

k) Steam for about 15-20 minutes or until the fish is cooked through.

l) Remove from the steaming pot and serve hot.

7. Khao Piak Sen - Rice noodle soup

Khao Piak Sen is a popular soup in Lao cuisine made of handmade rice noodles and chicken or pork broth. The noodles are cut to a short length and combined with broth that has been seasoned with fish sauce and herbs such as lemongrass, garlic, and cilantro. The soup is served with sliced meat, boiled egg, and vegetables such as bean sprouts and green onions. Khao Piak Sen is a hearty and comforting soup that is perfect for any occasion or weather.

Preparation Time: 25 min

Serving size: 2

Ingredients:

- 250g rice noodles
- 500ml chicken broth
- 200g chicken breast, sliced.
- 2 cloves garlic, minced.
- 1 tablespoon vegetable oil
- 1 tablespoon fish sauce
- 1 tablespoon soy sauce
- 1 teaspoon sugar
- 1/2 teaspoon black pepper
- 2 green onions, chopped.
- Fresh cilantro, for garnish

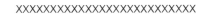

XXXXXXXXXXXXXXXXXXXXXXXXX

Instructions:

a) In a pot, cook the rice noodles according to the package instructions. Drain and set aside.

b) In the same pot, heat the vegetable oil over medium heat. Add the minced garlic and cook until fragrant.

c) Add the sliced chicken breast to the pot and cook until no longer pink.

d) Pour in the chicken broth and bring to a boil. Reduce heat and let simmer for 10 minutes.

e) Stir in the fish sauce, soy sauce, sugar, and black pepper. Taste and adjust seasoning if needed.

f) Divide the cooked rice noodles into two bowls. Ladle the soup over the noodles.

g) Garnish with chopped green onions and fresh cilantro.

h) Serve hot and enjoy!

8. Khao Jee - Baguette

Khao Jee, also known as Lao baguette, is a popular street food in Laos. Inspired by the French baguette, Khao Jee features a crispy yet soft bread with a light and airy texture. Traditionally filled with various ingredients such as grilled meat, pâté, pickled vegetables, and fresh herbs, Khao Jee is a savory and satisfying sandwich that offers a delicious blend of flavors and textures. It is the perfect handheld snack or meal on-the-go, showcasing the fusion of French and Lao culinary influences.

Preparation Time: 25 min

Serving size: 2

Ingredients:

- 1 baguette
- 2-3 slices of ham
- 2-3 slices of cheese (such as cheddar or Swiss)
- Mayonnaise
- Fresh cucumber thinly sliced.
- Fresh cilantro or parsley leaves

xxxxxxxxxxxxxxxxxxxxxxxxxx

Instructions:

a) Preheat your oven to 350°F (175°C).

b) Slice the baguette horizontally, lengthwise, creating a top and bottom half.

c) Spread a thin layer of mayonnaise on both sides of the baguette.

d) Layer the ham slices and cheese slices on the bottom half of the baguette.

e) Add the sliced cucumber on top of the cheese.

f) Top with fresh cilantro or parsley leaves for added freshness.

g) Place the baguette halves on a baking sheet and cover with aluminum foil.

h) Bake in the preheated oven for about 10-15 minutes, until the cheese is melted, and the baguette is warmed through.

i) Remove from the oven and let it cool slightly.

j) Press the top and bottom halves together and cut the baguette into individual sandwiches or slices.

k) Serve your Khao Jee baguette and enjoy it as a quick and tasty snack or light meal.

9. Khao Piak - Thick Rice Noodle Soup

Khao Piak is a filling and satisfying soup that is a staple in Lao cuisine. This traditional soup is made with a broth that has been simmered with chicken, pork, or beef bones, and seasoned with a mix of herbs and spices like lemongrass, garlic, and ginger. The soup is also filled with soft and chewy handmade rice flour noodles and served with sliced meat and vegetables such as green onions, cilantro, and bean sprouts. Khao Piak is a comforting and delicious soup perfect for any occasion.

Preparation Time: 25 min

Serving size: 2

Ingredients:

- 1 lb. boneless chicken thigh, sliced into small pieces.
- 1 onion, chopped.
- 4 garlic cloves, minced.
- 2 tablespoons oil
- 8 cups chicken broth
- 2 teaspoons fish sauce
- 1 teaspoon salt
- 1/2 teaspoon white pepper
- 1 package (16 oz) fresh or dried khao piak noodles
- 3-4 green onions thinly sliced.
- Fresh cilantro or parsley leaves, chopped.
- Fried garlic (optional)

xxxxxxxxxxxxxxxxxxxxxxxxx

Instructions:

a) Warm the oil in a big pot on medium heat. Put the chopped onion and minced garlic. Saute until fragrant and softened.

b) Add the sliced chicken and cook until the chicken is no longer pink.

c) Pour in the chicken broth and add the fish sauce, salt, and white pepper. Stir well to combine all the ingredients.

d) Bring the soup to a boil and then lower the heat to a simmer. Continue to cook for about 20-30 minutes, or until the chicken is cooked through.

e) While the soup is simmering, cook the khao piak noodles according to the package instructions. Drain and rinse with cold water to prevent the noodles from sticking together.

f) Add the cooked noodles to the pot of soup and stir well to combine.

g) Garnish the soup with sliced green onions, chopped cilantro or parsley leaves, and fried garlic (if using).

h) Serve your Khao Piak soup hot and enjoy its rich and comforting flavors.

10. Or Lam - Spicy Meat and Vegetable Soup

Or Lam is a traditional Lao stew that is rich in flavors and spices. This hearty dish is typically made with a combination of meat, such as pork or beef, and a variety of vegetables, such as eggplant, pumpkin, and green beans. It is seasoned with a blend of aromatic herbs and spices including galangal, lemongrass, and chili. The result is a thick and flavorful stew that can be enjoyed with sticky rice, providing a truly satisfying and delicious meal.

Preparation Time: 25 min

Serving size: 2

Ingredients:

- 500g meat (pork, beef, or chicken)
- 2 cups mixed vegetables (carrots, cabbage, green beans, etc.)
- 2 cups chicken or vegetable broth
- 2 tablespoons fish sauce
- 2 tablespoons lime juice
- 2 tablespoons chili paste.
- 1 tablespoon sugar
- 1 tablespoon oil
- Salt to taste

XXXXXXXXXXXXXXXXXXXXXXXXXX

Instructions:

a) Heat oil in a pot over medium heat.

b) Add the meat and cook until browned.

c) Add the mixed vegetables and cook for a few minutes.

d) Pour in the broth, fish sauce, lime juice, chili paste, sugar, and salt.

e) Stir well and bring to a boil.

f) Reduce heat and simmer for about 20 minutes, or until the vegetables are tender and the flavors have melded together.

g) Serve hot and enjoy!

11. Oua Si Khai - Stuffed lemongrass chicken wings

Oua Si Khai, also known as Lao stuffed lemongrass, is a popular appetizer in Lao cuisine. This flavorful dish consists of ground chicken or pork that is mixed with herbs and spices, stuffed into lemongrass stalks, and then grilled to perfection. The lemongrass imparts a citrusy and fragrant flavor to the meat, which is complemented by the savory and spicy seasonings. Oua Si Khai is a tasty and unique dish that is perfect for sharing with friends and family.

Preparation Time: 25 min

Serving size: 2

Ingredients:

- 10-12 chicken wings
- 2 stalks of lemongrass
- 1 tablespoon oyster sauce
- 1 tablespoon soy sauce
- 1 tablespoon fish sauce
- 1 teaspoon sugar
- 2 cloves of garlic, minced.
- 1/2 teaspoon black pepper
- Cooking oil for frying

XXXXXXXXXXXXXXXXXXXXXXXXXXX

Instructions:

a) Prepare the lemongrass by removing the tough outer layers and trimming off the top and bottom. Cut each stalk into 6-inch lengths.

b) Gently make an incision in each chicken wing, creating a pocket for the stuffing. Be careful not to cut through the other side.

c) In a mixing bowl, combine oyster sauce, soy sauce, fish sauce, sugar, minced garlic, and black pepper. Mix well to make the marinade.

d) Place the chicken wings in the marinade and ensure they are well coated. Cover the bowl and let the chicken marinate in the refrigerator for at least 30 minutes.

e) Take each piece of lemongrass and stuff it into the pocket of each chicken wing. This will add flavor and aroma to the wings.

f) Heat cooking oil in a deep pan or pot on medium-high heat.

g) Carefully decrease the stuffed chicken wings into the hot oil and fry until begin golden brown and cooked evenly, about 8-10 minutes.

h) Use tongs to unstick the chicken wings from the oil and transfer them to a paper towel-lined plate to drain excess oil.

i) Serve the Oua Si Khai - Stuffed Lemongrass Chicken Wings as a delicious appetizer or as part of a meal and enjoy the flavorful combination of lemongrass and tender chicken.

12. Jeow Mak Keua (Eggplant Dip)

Eggplant Dip (Jeow Mak Keua) is a flavorful and versatile Lao dish that showcases the smoky goodness of grilled eggplant. This dip combines charred eggplant with garlic, shallots, chili peppers, fish sauce, and lime juice for a tangy and spicy flavor profile. Served with sticky rice or as a condiment for meats and vegetables, Jeow Mak Keua adds a rich and savory element to any meal. It's a must-try for eggplant enthusiasts and lovers of bold flavors

Preparation Time: 25 min

Serving size: 2

Ingredients:

- 1 large eggplant
- 2 cloves garlic, minced.
- 2 small shallots, minced.
- 2-3 small red chili peppers, minced (or to taste)
- 3 tablespoons fish sauce
- 2 tablespoons lime juice
- 1 tablespoon brown sugar
- Salt to taste

xxxxxxxxxxxxxxxxxxxxxxxxx

Instructions:

a) Preheat a grill, stovetop grill pans or broiler on high heat.

b) Pierce the eggplant several times with a fork. Grill or broil eggplant until the skin is charred and the flesh is tender, about 15-20 minutes.

c) Remove eggplant from the heat and let it cool slightly. Remove and discard the charred skin and stem and place the eggplant flesh in a mixing bowl.

d) Add minced garlic, shallots, chili peppers, fish sauce, lime juice, brown sugar, and salt to the eggplant. Mix well and adjust the seasonings according to your preference.

e) Serve the Eggplant Dip (Jeow Mak Keua) with sticky rice, fresh vegetables, or cooked meats for dipping. Enjoy the smoky and savory flavors!

13. Sien Savanh - Lao-style beef jerky

Sien Savanh is a traditional Lao soup that is filled with aromatic flavors. It consists of hearty beef broth, tender beef slices, and an assortment of vegetables such as mushrooms, cabbage, and bean sprouts. The soup is seasoned with a combination of lemongrass, galangal, lime leaves, and fish sauce, giving it a tangy and savory taste. Sien Savanh is a comforting and satisfying dish that is enjoyed as a main course in Lao cuisine.

Preparation Time: 25 min

Serving size: 2

Ingredients:

- 1 lb. beef flank steak, thinly sliced against the grain.
- 1/2 cup fish sauce
- 1/4 cup soy sauce
- 1/4 cup brown sugar
- 1 tablespoon freshly ground black pepper.
- 4 cloves garlic, minced.
- 1/2 tablespoon paprika

XXXXXXXXXXXXXXXXXXXXXXXXXXX

Instructions:

a) In a bowl, whisk together the fish sauce, soy sauce, brown sugar, black pepper, minced garlic, and paprika.

b) Add the thinly sliced beef to the marinade and toss to coat. Marinate for at least 4 hours or overnight in the refrigerator.

c) Preheat your oven to 175°F (80°C) or the lowest temperature setting available.

d) Arrange the marinated beef slices on a wire rack set on top of a baking sheet.

e) Bake the beef jerky in the oven for 4-6 hours until dry and leathery, flipping once halfway through. Check the beef jerky after 4 hours and continue baking until dried to your liking.

f) Allow the beef jerky to cool completely before storing in an airtight container.

14. Sao Long - Grilled beef intestines

Sao Long, also known as grilled beef intestines, is a popular street food in Lao cuisine. The intestines are cleaned, marinated with herbs and spices, and then skewered before being grilled over charcoal until crispy and slightly charred. The result is a savory, chewy and flavorful dish that is rich in texture. It is often served with a dipping sauce made from chili, lime, and garlic, adding an extra tangy and spicy element of flavor to the dish.

Preparation Time: 25 min

Serving size: 2

Ingredients:

- 1 lb. beef intestines
- 1/4 cup fish sauce
- 1/4 cup soy sauce
- 2 tablespoons honey
- 1/2 tablespoon garlic powder
- 1/2 tablespoon onion powder
- 1 tablespoon freshly ground black pepper.
- 1/2 tablespoon paprika

xxxxxxxxxxxxxxxxxxxxxxxxx

Instructions:

a) In a bowl, whisk together the fish sauce, soy sauce, honey, black pepper, garlic powder, onion powder, and paprika.

b) Clean the beef intestines thoroughly and cut them into small pieces.

c) Add the pieces of beef intestines to the marinade and toss to coat. Marinate for at least 2 hours or overnight in the refrigerator.

d) Preheat your grill to medium-high heat.

e) Thread the beef intestines onto skewers.

f) Grill the skewers of beef intestines for 5-7 minutes per side, until charred and cooked through.

g) Serve the Sao Long hot off the grill with sticky rice, fresh herbs, and dipping sauce.

15. Taeng Gwa – Grilled Eggplant with Spicy Tomato Dipping Sauce

Taeng Gwa is a popular Lao dish that features stir-fried cucumber. The cucumbers are sliced and lightly sautéed in a hot pan along with other ingredients such as garlic, onions, and chili. The dish is seasoned with fish sauce, soy sauce, and a touch of sugar, creating a balance of savory and slightly sweet flavors. Taeng Gwa is a refreshing and flavorful dish that pairs well with rice or noodles in Lao cuisine.

Preparation Time: 25 min

Serving size: 2

Ingredients:

- 2 eggplants
- 2 tomatoes
- 2 cloves of garlic
- 1 red chili pepper
- 2 tablespoons of soy sauce
- 1 tablespoon of vinegar
- 1 tablespoon of sugar
- 1 tablespoon of sesame oil
- Salt to taste

XXXXXXXXXXXXXXXXXXXXXXXXXXX

Instructions:

a) Preheat the grill pan over medium heat.

b) Cut the eggplants into slices, about 1/2 inch thick.

c) Sprinkle salt over the eggplant slices and let them sit for 10 minutes to remove excess moisture.

d) In the meantime, prepare the spicy tomato dipping sauce. Blend the tomatoes, garlic, red chili pepper, soy sauce, vinegar, sugar, and sesame oil in a blender until smooth.

e) Grill the eggplant slices on the preheated grill pan for about 3-4 minutes on each side, or until they are cooked through and have grill marks.

f) Serve the grilled eggplant slices with the spicy tomato dipping sauce on the side.

g) Enjoy your Taeng Gwa - Grilled Eggplant with Spicy Tomato Dipping Sauce!

16. Jee Gai - Chicken noodle soup

Jee Gai is a flavorful and comforting chicken noodle soup in Lao cuisine. The soup is made by simmering chicken broth with tender chicken pieces, aromatic herbs like lemongrass and ginger, and spices such as star anise and cinnamon. The noodles, typically rice noodles, are added to the soup along with bean sprouts, cilantro, and green onions for added freshness and crunch. Jee Gai is a popular and satisfying dish that is perfect for warming up on a chilly day.

Preparation Time: 25 min

Serving size: 2

Ingredients:

- 1 lb. boneless, skinless chicken breasts thinly sliced.
- 6 cups chicken broth
- 2 cloves garlic, minced.
- 1 small onion, chopped.
- 2 carrots, sliced.
- 2 stalks celery, sliced.
- 4 ounces rice noodles or egg noodles
- 1 tablespoon fresh lime juice
- 2 tablespoons soy sauce or fish sauce
- Salt and pepper to taste.
- Fresh cilantro leaves for garnish (optional)

XXXXXXXXXXXXXXXXXXXXXXXXXX

Instructions:

a) In a big pot, warm some oil on medium heat. Put the minced garlic and chopped onion, and sauté for a few minutes until fragrant.

b) Add the sliced chicken breasts, carrots, and celery to the pot. Cook until the chicken is no longer pink, and the vegetables have softened slightly.

c) Pour in the chicken broth and bring to a boil. Reduce the heat and let it simmer for about 10-15 minutes.

d) In a separate pot, cook the rice noodles or egg noodles according to the package instructions. Drain and set aside.

e) Add soy sauce or fish sauce, fresh lime juice, salt, and pepper to the soup. Adjust the seasoning to your taste.

f) To serve, divide the cooked noodles among bowls and ladle the hot chicken soup over the noodles.

g) Garnish with fresh cilantro leaves, if desired. Enjoy your comforting bowl of Jee Gai!

17. Tom Kha Gai – Coconut milk soup with chicken

Tom Kha Gai is a delicious and creamy coconut milk soup with chicken that originates from Thai cuisine. The soup is made by simmering chicken in a fragrant broth of coconut milk, lemongrass, galangal, and kaffir lime leaves. It is then generously seasoned with fish sauce, lime juice, and Thai chili, giving it a perfect balance of sweet, sour, and spicy flavors. Tom Kha Gai is a popular and comforting soup that is enjoyed for its rich and aromatic taste.

Preparation Time: 25 min

Serving size: 2

Ingredients:

- 1 lb. boneless, skinless chicken breasts, thinly sliced.
- 3 cups chicken broth
- 2 cans (13.5 oz each) coconut milk
- 1 stalk lemongrass, bruised.
- 3-4 kaffir lime leaves
- 1 inch piece of galangal or ginger, sliced.
- 2 tablespoons fish sauce
- 2 tablespoons lime juice
- 2 tablespoons brown sugar
- 1 cup mushrooms, sliced.
- 1 small onion thinly sliced.
- Fresh cilantro leaves for garnish (optional)

XXXXXXXXXXXXXXXXXXXXXXXX

Instructions:

a) In a large pot, bring the chicken broth to a boil. Add the lemongrass, kaffir lime leaves, and galangal or ginger slices. Simmer for about 5-10 minutes to allow the flavors to infuse.

b) Reduce the heat to medium and add the chicken slices, mushrooms, and onion to the pot. Cook until the chicken is no longer pink and cooked through.

c) Stir in the coconut milk, fish sauce, lime juice, and brown sugar. Bring the soup back to a simmer and let it cook for another 5 minutes.

d) Remove the lemongrass stalk, kaffir lime leaves, and galangal or ginger slices from the soup.

e) Serve the Tom Kha Gai hot in bowls, garnished with fresh cilantro leaves if desired. Enjoy!

18. Mok Pa Khao - Steamed fish and rice in banana leaves

Mok Pa Khao is a traditional Lao dish that consists of steamed fish and rice wrapped in aromatic banana leaves. The fish is marinated with a combination of herbs and spices like lemongrass, galangal, and kaffir lime leaves. It is then cooked by steaming in the banana leaves, which infuses the fish with a delightful aroma. The rice is often mixed with vegetables and placed alongside the fish. Mok Pa Khao is a flavorful and visually appealing dish that showcases the rich culinary heritage of Laos.

Preparation Time: 25 min

Serving size: 2

Ingredients:

- 2 fish fillets
- 2 cups of cooked
- 4 banana leaves

XXXXXXXXXXXXXXXXXXXXXXXXXXX

Instructions:

a) Place the fish fillets on the banana leaves.

b) Add cooked rice on top of the fish fillets.

c) Wrap the banana leaves around the fish and rice, creating a parcel.

d) Place the parcels in a steamer and steam for 20 minutes.

e) Serve hot and enjoy.

19. Khao Soy - Northern-style coconut curry noodle soup

Khao Soy is a delicious and aromatic noodle soup that originates from northern Thailand. It is a rich and creamy coconut curry-based soup that is served with both egg noodles and crispy fried noodles on top. The soup is flavored with fragrant spices such as turmeric and ginger, along with a hint of sweetness from palm sugar. It is commonly garnished with lime wedges, pickled mustard greens, shallots, and crispy shallots. Khao Soy is a popular and comforting dish that is bursting with layers of flavors and textures.

Preparation Time: 25 min

Serving size: 2

Ingredients:

- 2 tablespoons vegetable oil
- 1 small onion thinly sliced.
- 3 cloves garlic, minced.
- 2 tablespoons red curry paste
- 1 can (400 ml) coconut milk
- 2 cups chicken or vegetable broth
- 2 tablespoons fish sauce
- 1 tablespoon sugar
- 200 grams boneless chicken thighs, sliced.
- 200 grams egg noodles, cooked.
- For garnish: chopped cilantro, lime wedges, sliced shallots, crispy noodles.

xxxxxxxxxxxxxxxxxxxxxxxxx

Instructions:

a) Heat the vegetable oil in a large pot over medium heat.

b) Add the sliced onion and minced garlic and cook until softened.

c) Stir in the red curry paste and cook for 1-2 minutes.

d) Pour in the coconut milk and chicken or vegetable broth. Bring to a simmer.

e) Add the fish sauce and sugar and stir to combine.

f) Add the sliced chicken thighs and cook until cooked through.

g) Divide the cooked egg noodles into serving bowls.

h) Ladle the soup over the noodles.

i) Garnish with chopped cilantro, lime wedges, sliced shallots, and crispy noodles.

j) Serve hot and enjoy!

20. Pho Lao - Lao-style pho noodle soup

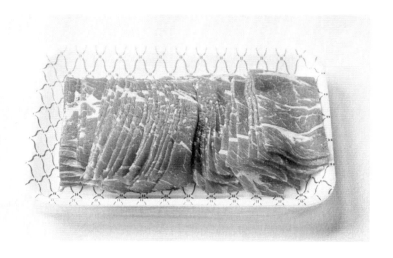

Pho Lao is a flavorful and aromatic noodle soup that is inspired by the traditional Vietnamese dish, pho. It is a popular dish in Lao cuisine, with its own unique twist. The soup is made by simmering a rich and fragrant broth with various herbs and spices such as star anise, cinnamon, and cloves. Thin rice noodles are added to the soup, along with thinly sliced beef or chicken, bean sprouts, and fresh herbs. Pho Lao is a comforting and satisfying dish that embodies the harmonious blend of flavors in Lao cuisine.

Preparation Time: 25 min

Serving size: 2

Ingredients:

- 1 lb. beef sirloin thinly sliced.
- 8 cups beef broth
- 1 cinnamon stick
- 4-star anise pods
- 4 cloves
- 1 teaspoon coriander seeds
- 1 onion, sliced.
- 2 tablespoons fish sauce
- 1 tablespoon soy sauce
- 8 ounces rice noodles
- Bean sprouts, basil leaves, lime wedges, and sliced chili peppers for garnish

xxxxxxxxxxxxxxxxxxxxxxxxxxx

Instructions:

a) In a large pot, dry roast the cinnamon stick, star anise pods, cloves, and coriander seeds over medium heat until fragrant. Remove the spices from the pot and set aside.

b) In the same pot, add the sliced onion and cook until softened and slightly caramelized.

c) Pour in the beef broth and add the roasted spices back into the pot. Bring to a boil and let it simmer for about 20-30 minutes to allow the flavors to combine.

d) While the broth is simmering, prepare the rice noodles according to the package instructions. Drain and set aside.

e) Remove the roasted spices from the pot using a slotted spoon or a strainer.

f) Stir the fish sauce and soy sauce into the soup. Adjust the seasoning to your taste.

g) To serve, divide the cooked rice noodles among bowls and ladle the hot beef broth over the noodles.

h) Arrange the thinly sliced beef sirloin on top of the hot broth.

i) Garnish with bean sprouts, basil leaves, lime wedges, and sliced chili peppers. Enjoy your delicious bowl of Pho Lao!

21. Khaiphaen - Fried River weed

Khaiphaen, also known as fried river weed, is a popular and unique snack that originates from the rivers of Laos. It is made by harvesting and drying edible river algae, which is then deep-fried until crispy. The result is a savory and crunchy snack that can be enjoyed on its own or as a topping for salads and other dishes. Khaiphaen is often seasoned with salt, garlic, and other herbs, adding a burst of flavor to this delectable treat.

Preparation Time: 25 min

Serving size: 2

Ingredients:

- 1 river weed

Instructions:

a) Heat a frying pan.

b) Add the river weed to the pan.

c) Fry the river weed for 25 minutes, or until crispy.

d) Remove the fried river weed from the pan and let it cool.

e) Serve the fried river weed as a snack or side dish.

22. Lao Pork Curry (Gaeng Moo)

Lao Pork Curry, or Gaeng Moo, is a traditional Lao dish known for its rich flavors and spicy kick. The dish features tender chunks of pork that are simmered in a flavorful curry paste made from a blend of aromatic herbs and spices. The addition of coconut milk adds a creamy and comforting touch to the dish. It's typically served alongside steamed rice and is a satisfying and delicious meal that warms the belly and soul.

Preparation Time: 25 min

Serving size: 2

Ingredients:

- 1 pound pork shoulder, cut into bite-sized pieces.
- 2 tablespoons vegetable oil
- 2 tablespoons Lao curry paste
- 1 can coconut milk (13.5 ounces)
- 1 cup water
- 1 tablespoon fish sauce
- 1 tablespoon sugar
- 1 carrot, sliced.
- 1 bell pepper, sliced.
- Fresh Thai basil leaves, for garnish
- Cooked rice, for serving.

XXXXXXXXXXXXXXXXXXXXXXXXXX

Instructions:

a) In a large pot, heat the vegetable oil over medium heat. Add the curry paste and cook for a few minutes until fragrant.

b) Add the pork shoulder to the pot and cook until browned on all sides.

c) Pour in the coconut milk and water. Stir well to combine.

d) Add the fish sauce and sugar, then let the curry simmer for about 45 minutes to 1 hour until the pork becomes tender.

e) Add the sliced carrot and bell pepper to the pot and cook for an additional 5-10 minutes until the vegetables become tender.

f) Garnish the curry with fresh Thai basil leaves.

g) Serve the Lao Pork Curry over cooked rice. Enjoy the flavorful and spicy curry!

23. Som Moo - Sour pork sausage

Som Moo is a traditional Lao delicacy that features sour pork sausage. Made from fermented ground pork, the sausage is seasoned with a mixture of herbs, spices, and salt to enhance the flavors. The fermentation process gives Som Moo a tangy and slightly sour taste that pairs perfectly with sticky rice or as an accompaniment to other Lao dishes. The sausage is often grilled or pan-fried, resulting in a deliciously crispy exterior and a moist, flavorful interior. Som Moo is a staple in Lao cuisine and a must-try for those seeking authentic Lao flavors.

Preparation Time: 25 min

Serving size: 2

Ingredients:

- 1 lb. ground pork
- 2 tablespoons cooked sticky rice.
- 2 teaspoons red curry paste
- 1 teaspoon salt
- 1 tablespoon sugar
- 2 tablespoons fish sauce
- 2 tablespoons lime juice
- 3-4 bird's eye chilies thinly sliced.
- 1/4 cup sliced shallots.
- Fresh herbs (such as cilantro, mint, or Thai basil) for garnish

xxxxxxxxxxxxxxxxxxxxxxxxx

Instructions:

a) In a mixing bowl, combine the ground pork, cooked sticky rice, red curry paste, salt, sugar, fish sauce, lime juice, bird's eye chilies, and sliced shallots. Mix well to combine all the ingredients.

b) Cover the bowl and let the mixture marinate in the refrigerator for at least 2 hours, or overnight for best results.

c) Shape the marinated pork mixture into small sausage-shaped patties or logs, about 2-3 inches long.

d) Heat a grill or non-stick skillet over medium heat. Cook the Som Moo sausages until they are browned and cooked through, about 4-5 minutes per side.

e) Once cooked, transfer the Som Moo sausages to a serving plate.

f) Garnish with fresh herbs such as cilantro, mint, or Thai basil. Serve the Som Moo hot as an appetizer or as part of a meal. Enjoy!

24. Orlam Gai - Chicken stew with vegetables and herbs

Orlam Gai is a delicious and aromatic chicken stew that is packed with wholesome vegetables and fragrant herbs. This traditional dish is an absolute delight for the taste buds. Tender chicken pieces are simmered in a flavorful broth along with a variety of fresh vegetables like carrots, bell peppers, and mushrooms. The stew is then infused with aromatic herbs and spices, creating a comforting and hearty meal that is perfect for any occasion. Orlam Gai is a true culinary delight that will leave you craving for more.

Preparation Time: 25 min

Serving size: 2

Ingredients:

- 2 chicken breasts
- 1 onion
- 2 cloves of garlic
- 1 carrot
- 1 bell pepper
- 1 zucchini
- 1 cup of chicken broth
- 1 tablespoon of olive oil
- 1 teaspoon of dried thyme
- 1 teaspoon of dried rosemary
- Salt and pepper to taste.

xxxxxxxxxxxxxxxxxxxxxxxxxx

Instructions:

a) Heat the olive oil in a large pot over medium heat.

b) Chop the onion, garlic, carrot, bell pepper, and zucchini.

c) Add the chopped vegetables to the pot and sauté for 5 minutes.

d) Cut the chicken breasts into bite-sized pieces and add them to the pot.

e) Cook the chicken until it is no longer pink.

f) Add the chicken broth, dried thyme, dried rosemary, salt, and pepper to the pot.

g) Stir everything together and bring the stew to a simmer.

h) Let the stew simmer for 15 minutes, or until the vegetables are tender.

i) Serve the Orlam Gai stew hot and enjoy!

25. Koi - Steamed Seaweed with Sesame and Garlic

Koi is a popular and healthy dish that features steamed seaweed coated with a tasty mixture of sesame and garlic. This traditional dish is a staple in many Asian cuisines, and it is known for its unique blend of textures and flavors. The soft, delicate seaweed is balanced with the nutty aroma of sesame seeds and the pungent kick of garlic. Koi is a simple yet flavorful dish that is perfect as a light appetizer or a side dish to accompany your favorite Asian meal.

Preparation Time: 25 min

Serving size: 2

Ingredients:

- 1 cup dried seaweed (such as wakame or kombu)
- 2 tablespoons sesame oil
- 2 garlic cloves, minced.
- 1 tablespoon soy sauce
- 1 teaspoon sugar
- 1 tablespoon toasted sesame seeds
- Sliced green onions for garnish.

XXXXXXXXXXXXXXXXXXXXXXXXX

Instructions:

a) Soak the dried seaweed in cold water for about 10 minutes, or until it becomes soft and pliable.

b) Drain the soaked seaweed and pat it dry with a clean towel.

c) In a small bowl, combine the sesame oil, minced garlic, soy sauce, and sugar. Mix well to make the dressing.

d) Place the seaweed in a heatproof bowl or dish that fits inside a steamer basket.

e) Pour the dressing over the seaweed, making sure it is evenly coated.

f) Sprinkle the toasted sesame seeds over the seaweed.

g) Fill a steamer pot with water and bring it to a boil.

h) Place the bowl or dish with the seaweed in the steamer basket and steam for about 5 minutes, or until the seaweed is tender.

i) Carefully remove the steamed seaweed from the steamer and transfer it to a serving plate.

j) Garnish with sliced green onions. Serve the Koi as a side dish or as part of a larger meal. Enjoy!

26. Pa Tong Go - Fried dough sticks

Pa Tong Go, also known as fried dough sticks, is a popular snack in many Asian cuisines, including Thai and Chinese. These crispy and golden sticks are made by deep-frying a dough mixture until they become light and fluffy on the inside while developing a crunchy exterior. Pa Tong Go is often enjoyed for breakfast or as a snack, served with a dipping sauce like sweetened condensed milk or soy sauce. These addictive treats are perfect for those craving something crispy, doughy, and delicious.

Preparation Time: 25 min

Serving size: 2

Ingredients:

- 2 cups all-purpose flour
- 1 tablespoon sugar
- 1 teaspoon salt
- 1 tablespoon baking powder
- 1/2 cup warm water
- Vegetable oil for deep frying

xxxxxxxxxxxxxxxxxxxxxxxxxx

Instructions:

a) In a mixing bowl, combine the all-purpose flour, sugar, salt, and baking powder. Mix well to combine all the dry ingredients.

b) Add the warm water to the dry mixture, stir with a spoon or spatula until the dough comes together.

c) Knead the dough for about 3-5 minutes until it becomes smooth and elastic and place it into a clean bowl. Cover with a lid or plastic wrap and let it rest for at least 30 minutes.

d) Once rested, divide the dough into small pieces, about 2 inches long. Roll each piece of dough into a long strip.

e) Heat the vegetable oil in a wok or deep-frying pan over medium heat.

f) Gently place each dough strip into the hot oil and fry until golden brown, turning occasionally to cook evenly on all sides.

g) Once cooked, remove the Pa Tong Go from the oil and place them on a paper towel to drain off any excess oil.

h) Serve the warm Pa Tong Go with your choice of dipping sauce, such as sweetened condensed milk or pandan custard. Enjoy!

27. Tom Yum - Spicy and Sour Soup

Tom Yum is well-known and beloved with a powerful flavor profile of spicy and sour notes. Made with a combination of aromatic herbs and spices, such as lemongrass, kaffir lime leaves, and chili peppers, the soup is bursting with bold flavors. Packed with fresh ingredients like shrimp, mushrooms, and sometimes chicken or tofu, Tom Yum is a delightful dish that will tantalize your taste buds and leave you craving for more. It's a perfect choice for those who enjoy a spicy and tangy culinary experience.

Preparation Time: 25 min

Serving size: 2

Ingredients:

- 2 cups vegetable broth
- 1 stalk lemongrass
- 3 kaffir lime leaves
- 2 slices galangal
- 2 Thai chilies
- 1 tomato
- 4 button mushrooms
- 1/2 cup tofu
- 2 tablespoons fish sauce
- 2 tablespoons lime juice
- 1 teaspoon sugar
- 1/4 cup cilantro

xxxxxxxxxxxxxxxxxxxxxxxxx

Instructions:

a) In a pot, bring the vegetable broth to a boil.

b) Bruise the lemongrass stalk and add it to the pot along with the kaffir lime leaves and galangal slices.

c) Slice the Thai chilies and tomato and add them to the pot.

d) Cut the button mushrooms and tofu into bite-sized pieces and add them to the pot.

e) Stir in the fish sauce, lime juice, and sugar.

f) Let the soup simmer for 15 minutes.

g) Garnish with cilantro before serving.

28. Khao Poon - Spicy vermicelli soup

Khao Poon is a flavorful and spicy vermicelli soup that is popular in Laos cuisine. Made with a rich and fragrant broth, the soup features thin rice noodles that are cooked to perfection. Infused with a combination of aromatic herbs and spices, including lemongrass, galangal, and chili, Khao Poon is known for its spicy kick. It is commonly served with an array of toppings such as shredded chicken, herbs, bean sprouts, and lime. This bold and satisfying soup is a must-try for those seeking a spicy and aromatic culinary adventure.

Preparation Time: 25 min

Serving size: 2

Ingredients:

- 1-pound boneless chicken thighs, sliced
- 3 tablespoons red curry paste
- 2 cans coconut milk (13.5 ounces each)
- 4 cups chicken broth
- 2 tablespoons fish sauce
- 1 tablespoon sugar
- 1 red bell pepper, sliced.
- 1 cup sliced mushrooms.
- 1 cup fresh bean sprouts
- 1 lime, juiced.
- 1/4 cup chopped cilantro.
- Cooked vermicelli noodles, for serving.

xxxxxxxxxxxxxxxxxxxxxxxxxx

Instructions:

a) In a large pot, heat some oil over medium heat and add the red curry paste. Cook for a few minutes until the paste becomes fragrant.

b) Add the sliced chicken thighs to the pot and cook until they are no longer pink.

c) Pour in the coconut milk and chicken broth. Stir well to combine.

d) Add the fish sauce and sugar. Stir again to mix everything together.

e) Bring the soup to a simmer and let it cook for about 10 minutes.

f) Add the sliced bell pepper and mushrooms to the pot and cook for an additional 5 minutes until the vegetables become tender.

g) Stir in the bean sprouts and lime juice. Cook for another minute or two.

h) Remove the pot from the heat and sprinkle the chopped cilantro over the soup.

i) Serve the Khao Poon soup over cooked vermicelli noodles. Enjoy the flavorful and spicy vermicelli soup!

29. Kua Mee - Stir-fried noodles

Kua Mee is a delicious, stir-fried noodle dish. Made with a variety of noodles, such as rice noodles or egg noodles, the dish is stir-fried with a medley of fresh vegetables and your choice of protein, such as chicken, beef, or tofu. The noodles are infused with savory flavors from a combination of sauces and seasonings, creating a harmonious blend of tastes and textures. Kua Mee is a satisfying and multipurpose dish that can be enjoyed as a main course or even side dish.

Preparation Time: 25 min

Serving size: 2

Ingredients:

- 8 ounces dried rice noodles
- 2 tablespoons vegetable oil
- 2 cloves garlic, minced.
- 6-8 large shrimp peeled and deveined.
- 1/4-pound boneless pork sliced thinly.
- 2 eggs, beaten.
- 2 tablespoons oyster sauce
- 1 tablespoon soy sauce
- 1 tablespoon sugar
- 1/2 onion sliced thinly.
- 1/2 cup bean sprouts
- 1/4 cup scallions sliced thinly.
- Lime wedges, for serving.

XXXXXXXXXXXXXXXXXXXXXXXXXXX

Instructions:

a) Soak the dried rice noodles in hot water for about 10-15 minutes until softened. Drain and set aside.

b) Heat a wok or large skillet over high heat and add the vegetable oil. Once hot, add the minced garlic and cook until fragrant.

c) Add the shrimp and sliced pork to the wok and cook for a few minutes until the shrimp becomes pink and the pork becomes browned.

d) Add the beaten eggs to the wok and scramble until the eggs are fully cooked.

e) Add the oyster sauce, soy sauce, and sugar to the wok and stir well to combine all the ingredients.

f) Add in the sliced onion, bean sprouts, and scallions, and cook for a few minutes until the vegetables are tender.

g) Add the soaked rice noodles to the wok and toss everything until the noodles are coated in sauce and everything is heated through.

h) Serve the Kua Mee hot with lime wedges on the side for squeezing over the top. Enjoy your delicious, stir-fried noodles!

30. Khao Poon Nam Phik - Spicy Coconut Curry Noodle Soup

Khao Poon Nam Phik is a flavorful and creamy noodle soup that combines the richness of coconut curry with a spicy kick. Originating from Laos cuisine, this soup features thick rice noodles immersed in a fragrant broth made with red curry paste, coconut milk, and various aromatic herbs and spices. The soup is traditionally garnished with an array of toppings, such as shredded chicken, herbs, crispy fried shallots, and lime. Khao Poon Nam Phik is a must-try for those craving a spicy, creamy, and satisfying soup experience.

Preparation Time: 25 min

Serving size: 2

Ingredients:

- 200g rice vermicelli noodles
- 400ml coconut milk
- 2 cups vegetable broth
- 1 tablespoon red curry paste
- 1 tablespoon fish sauce
- 1 tablespoon sugar
- 1 lime, juiced.
- 200g chicken breast, thinly sliced.
- 100g shrimp, peeled and deveined.
- 1 red bell pepper, sliced.
- 1 carrot, julienned.
- 1/4 cup fresh cilantro, chopped.
- 1/4 cup green onions, sliced.

xxxxxxxxxxxxxxxxxxxxxxxxxx

Instructions:

a) Cook the rice vermicelli noodles following the package instructions. Drain and set aside.

b) In a pot, heat the coconut milk and vegetable broth over medium heat.

c) Add the red curry paste, fish sauce, sugar, and lime juice to the pot. Stir well to combine.

d) Add the chicken breast, shrimp, red bell pepper, and carrot to the pot. Cook until the chicken is cooked through, and the shrimp is pink.

e) Divide the cooked rice vermicelli noodles between two serving bowls.

f) Ladle the spicy coconut curry soup over the noodles.

g) Garnish with fresh cilantro and green onions.

h) Serve hot and enjoy!

My Words

I cannot express enough how grateful I am for your decision to purchase my book. It is a humbling feeling to know that people are interested in learning from my experiences and the content that I have created. Being a writer has allowed me to share my knowledge and skills with others, and it is truly an honor to have you choose my book out of the multitude of books available on the market.

Your choice to invest in my book is incredibly special to me, and I am confident that the content you will find within its pages will prove to be valuable and insightful. It is my sincere hope that you will learn a great deal from the knowledge I have shared and that it will positively impact your life in some way.

After reading the book, I kindly request that you leave feedback, no matter how small. As a writer, I am always looking to improve and provide better content to my readers. Your feedback will be an invaluable source of information, and I will take it into consideration when creating future books. It is my goal to create content that my readers love and find helpful, and your input will play an important role in helping me achieve that.

Once again, I would like to express my gratitude for your support and for choosing my book. Your investment in my work means the world to me, and I am honored to have the opportunity to share my knowledge with you. Your feedback and support will be greatly appreciated and will help me to continue creating meaningful and valuable content for readers like you.

Kind regards,

Alex Aton

Manufactured by Amazon.ca
Acheson, AB

11677470R00052